ME AND MY HORSE

Learning to Ride

Toni Webber

COPPER BEECH BOOKS
Brookfield, Connecticut

© Aladdin Books Ltd 2002

Produced by:
Aladdin Books Ltd
28 Percy Street
London W1T 2BZ

ISBN 0-7613-2752-5

First published in the United States in 2002 by:
Copper Beech Books,
an imprint of
The Millbrook Press
2 Old New Milford Road
Brookfield, Connecticut 06804

Editor:
Harriet Brown

Designers:
Flick, Book Design & Graphics
Simon Morse

Photography:
Aubrey Wade

Illustrators:
Terry Riley, Stephen Sweet, James Field, and Chris Tomlin—SGA
Steve Roberts—Wildlife Art Agency

Cartoons: Simon Morse

Certain illustrations have appeared in earlier books created by Aladdin Books.

Printed in U.A.E.
All rights reserved

Cataloging-in-Publication data is on file at the Library of Congress.

Contents

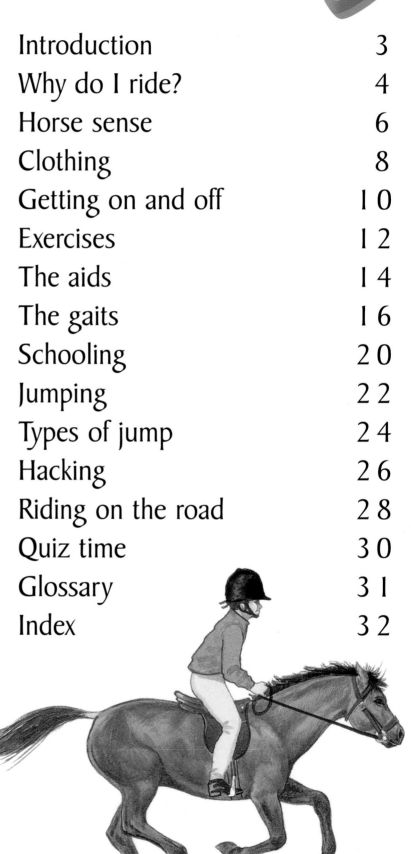

Introduction

Learning to Ride is a lively guide, which provides the information you need to help you get the most out of horses and riding. There are always new things to learn and new activities to try with your horse. This book will help you master the basics. You may go on to more advanced activities like show jumping, cross-country, and dressage. Or you may simply enjoy riding in the countryside, making friends, and having fun!

Follow Oscar and me as we learn to ride and have fun together —and do our best not to get into too much trouble!

Always Remember:
Look in these boxes for further information about learning to ride. They contain important points that you should try to remember.

THE RIGHTS AND WRONGS
Look out for these check boxes, as they show you how to do things correctly. Just as important, look out for the "X" boxes. These show you how not to do things.

Q What are these boxes for?

A These question and answer panels are here to help answer any questions you may have about horses and riding. They are on subjects relevant to the rest of the page they're on.

Follow my horse diary to find out about my riding progress —it could be a lot like yours! Why not make your own horse diary to keep track of your riding skills? It could help you remember all the fun you have with horses and new friends as you learn to ride.

Why do I ride?

In the past, horses and ponies were used as a form of transportation, to deliver messages, and to pull plows and carts—they were even sent down coal mines. Over the years, these intelligent animals have been highly trained. Today, hundreds of thousands of people all over the world enjoy riding horses and ponies. As you learn to ride you will make friends, have fun, and get to explore a lot of the countryside around you.

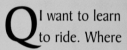

YOU AND YOUR HORSE

Horses and ponies are beautiful creatures. If they are well cared for they can give you affection, loyalty, fun, and excitement.

Q I want to learn to ride. Where can I find someone to teach me?

A In the US, most riding schools have some sort of official approval, which you should always look out for. Your local Pony Club or your town recreation office may be able to recommend a good riding school. If you see children in riding clothes, stop and ask where they ride. Even if they have their own horses, there may be someone there who is qualified to teach you.

Q Do horses make friends with each other and with people?

A Horses are herd animals and can form strong bonds with each other. They groom one another as a mother would groom her foal. You can make friends with your horse. As you get to know each other over time you can build a special, trusting relationship.

TRAINING

Training a horse to carry a rider used to be called "breaking in." Sometimes that meant literally breaking its spirit so that it was too scared to be anything other than obedient. Today, we know that to train a horse and to enjoy riding, you must trust each other.

Saturday
Woke up really early this morning because I was so excited to be going for my first riding lesson. It has taken ages to persuade Mom that this was all I have ever wanted to do. I was nervous to start with. They put me on a pony called Oscar, who is really beautiful. It was great—the instructor said I had a "natural seat!"

MAKING FRIENDS

One of the great things about riding is making friends. If you go to a riding stables, there are likely to be others of your age also learning to ride. At some riding stables you can get free lessons in return for helping out. Some people even spend the whole school vacation helping out at the stables.

Horse sense

Horses like company. In a field they will happily live with horses or other grazing animals, such as sheep, cows, or goats. They communicate using body language and facial expressions. By watching a horse, you can learn to understand what it is thinking.

Sunday
My instructor asked me if I wanted to help her get Oscar from the field before my lesson. He was miles away in the far corner. I walked straight toward him and just as I got near, he ran off in the other direction! I think I must have scared him.

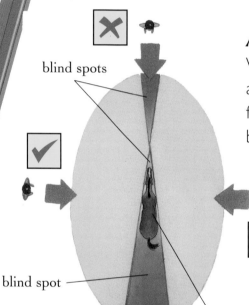

blind spots

blind spot

horse

APPROACHING YOUR HORSE
When you go up to a horse, always approach from the front and at an angle. This is because a horse's eyes are positioned so that it cannot see anything directly in front or behind. Talk to your horse as you approach.

Always Remember:
Be careful when handling sensitive areas. The belly can be a ticklish spot, and you should only use a soft body brush to remove mud and dirt. Clean the eyes and nostrils with a sponge that has been rinsed out in clean water. Use a separate sponge for cleaning the dock area (under the tail).

PICKING UP LEGS
Stand at a right angle to the horse, and run your hand down the back of the leg. Lean your body against the horse to encourage it to shift its weight onto the other leg. When your hand reaches the fetlock (just above the hoof), pull the foot up. Support the hoof in the palm of your hand.

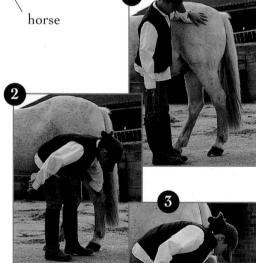

Q Do horses lie down to sleep?

A Horses and ponies usually sleep standing up. That way, horses in the wild can escape quickly in case of danger. Many horses do lie down to sleep from time to time.

Q Is it normal for my horse to rest its leg?

A Resting a hind leg is a common sign of drowsiness. If your horse rests a front foot, this may mean that it has an ailment called laminitis, and you should seek advice.

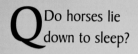

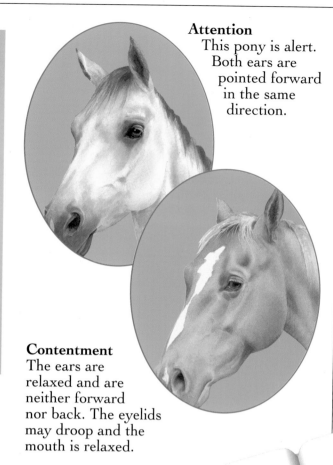

Attention
This pony is alert. Both ears are pointed forward in the same direction.

Contentment
The ears are relaxed and are neither forward nor back. The eyelids may droop and the mouth is relaxed.

HORSE BODY LANGUAGE

When your horse is interested in something, it arches its neck, pricks up its ears, and snorts. If your horse is warning you not to come too close, it may turn its rump toward you. Watching horses closely will help you to understand their language.

Anger
The ears are laid flat back, the nostrils are flared, and the mouth is open, ready to bite.

Fear
The ears are back, the eyes are rolled back to show a lot of white, and the nostrils are flared.

Later
My instructor said that next time I try to catch Oscar in the field I should watch his ears. Apparently they can tell you a lot about how he is feeling. I'll definitely make sure I talk to him as well so that he knows I'm there— I don't want him running off again!

Clothing

The two most important items of riding clothing are your hat and your boots. The hat must meet safety requirements and the boots must have a small heel. Warmth and comfort are very important. If you are likely to be riding on the road, you should make sure that you can be seen easily. You do not have to wear a formal riding jacket except on special occasions, but try to look as neatly dressed as you can.

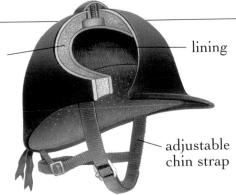

absorbent padding

lining

adjustable chin strap

YOUR RIDING HAT

Hats are either velvet covered with a built-in peak, or a helmet without a peak. These helmets are often covered with a black or colored silk. Both types have straps that fasten under your chin. Get an expert to make sure your hat is a good fit. Always ride with your chinstrap fastened.

BE SEEN!

You should always wear light or brightly colored clothing when riding on the road in daylight. At dusk or in the early morning, reflective clothing is essential. It is a good idea for your horse to wear a fluorescent exercise rug, boots, and bandages.

Oscar

Sunday

It was very windy and rainy today. I thought we would stay in the school, but they said we could go for a hack. Luckily I had my new wax riding coat—and so I stayed really dry—and Oscar had his fluorescent exercise rug so we showed up really well.

ST

THE RIGHT GEAR

This rider is dressed for a formal riding occasion. She is wearing jodhpurs, jodhpur boots, shirt, jacket, and most importantly, a riding hat.

hat

jacket

JODHPURS

Jodhpurs are stretchy, to let you move easily and are padded at the knee, to stop rubbing. They come in lots of colors, but beige and gray are most commonly used when dressing for shows.

jodhpurs

jodhpur boots

BOOTS

All riding boots should have a smooth sole and a small, defined heel. Jodhpur boots are short and made of brown or black leather. They reach to just above the ankle. An elastic insert makes them easy to get on and off. Knee-length riding boots are mainly used for special occasions.

Mustn't forget to clean my riding coat and jodhpurs tonight or Mom will go crazy —they have horse hair all over them!

THE WRONG GEAR

This girl would be unsafe out riding. Rubber boots have ridged soles and her feet could get stuck in the stirrups if she fell. A cap won't protect her head.

GLOVES

Riding gloves have grips on the palms and fingers. The gloves help stop your fingers from slipping on wet reins and keep your hands warm in winter.

Always Remember:

Cover up well in wet and windy weather. Some riding coats have a hood that fits over your riding hat and a skirt big enough to spread out behind you. This is held in place by straps that go under your thighs. These help to stop it from flapping around and startling your horse.
If you want to protect your horse, you could use a waterproof exercise rug.

Getting on and off

Before you go riding, you have to get on your horse, and when you have finished, you have to get off. This sounds very obvious, but there are ways of doing both that are safe for you and comfortable for your horse. Soon you will be able do both without even thinking about it.

pommel

1 Stand at your horse's near (left) side, by its shoulder, and face the rear. Pick up the reins in your left hand and hold the pommel. Put your left foot into the stirrup iron.

STIRRUP LEATHER LENGTH

Make a fist and place your knuckles against the stirrup bar. If the leathers are the right length, the bottom of the iron should reach your armpit.

2 Hold the cantle (back) of the saddle and spring upward. Swing your right leg over the back of the saddle.

3 Lower yourself gently into the saddle, and find the right stirrup with your right foot. Take the reins in both hands and check that your girth is tight.

cantle

girth

6 pm
My friend Annabel and I were fooling around today. First, we shortened our stirrups and pretended we were riding in the Grand National, and then we lengthened them so that we looked like knights of old. We didn't have much control either way. It's a good thing our ponies are so good.

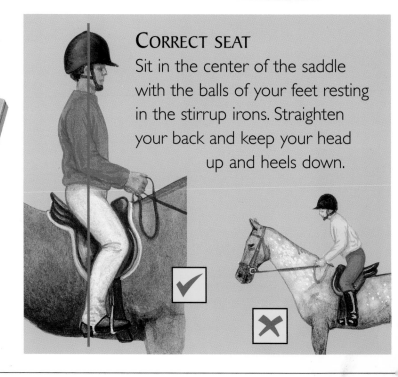

CORRECT SEAT

Sit in the center of the saddle with the balls of your feet resting in the stirrup irons. Straighten your back and keep your head up and heels down.

HOLDING THE REINS AND THE WHIP

The rein should pass between your third finger and little finger of each hand. Your thumb should be on top of the rein. The loop of slack rein hangs down the horse's left shoulder. It is sometimes useful to be able to ride one-handed. To do this with your left hand, for example, take the other rein in that hand and let it pass between your index and middle fingers (see left).

The rider in this picture (left) is holding the reins incorrectly and has little control.

This rider (right) is holding the reins correctly. He can send instant messages to the horse by moving his wrist and tightening his fingers.

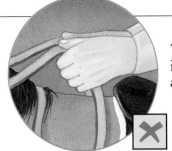

To hold a whip correctly, grip it lightly near the top with the lower part of it resting against your thigh (right).

Q Should my stirrups be the same length for all kinds of riding?

A No. When jumping, it is best to shorten your leathers by one or two holes. This will improve your jumping position. It is also a good idea to change your leathers from side to side occasionally. This gives your leathers a chance to stretch evenly as most riders ride more heavily on one side than the other.

4 To get off, wait until your horse is standing still. Hold the reins taut to keep a contact with its mouth, and remove both feet from the stirrups. Hold the pommel with your right hand.

6 Land lightly on both feet. Turn to face the front and be ready to stop your horse from moving on by placing your right hand on the rein.

I tried vaulting onto Oscar like they do in mounted games. I thought it would save a lot of time but I was hopeless!

5 Lean forward slightly and swing your right leg back and over the saddle. Support yourself on your tummy and right hand.

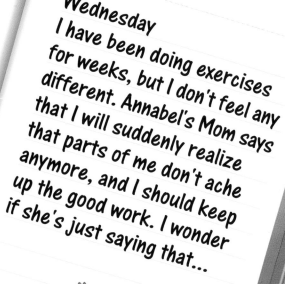

Exercises

Riding is all about balance, suppleness, and flexibility. When you ride, you use muscles that are not otherwise often used. You can develop your muscles by doing exercises. This will give you more control over your body and you won't ache as much.

ARM CIRCLING

Take your feet out of the stirrups and swing one arm in a wide circle, six times in one direction and six in the other. Then repeat the exercise with your other arm.

BACKWARD AND FORWARD

Keep your arms at your sides and lie back until your head is on your horse's rump. Then, fold forward so that your nose is near your horse's neck. Each time, return to the sitting position without using your arms to help you.

HEAD EXERCISES

Neck muscles can get very tired. You can tone them up by rotating your neck in a figure-eight movement. Do this about eight times. Never continue any exercise for too long. A short but regular session is best.

TOUCH TOES

Keeping one arm straight, raise it above your head. Bend at the waist and touch your toes on the opposite side with the tips of your fingers. Do the same with the other arm. This will help to make your body supple.

AROUND THE WORLD

This is a popular exercise for new riders; it helps to improve your balance. There should always be someone on foot, holding the horse when you are doing the exercise.

Always Remember:

Keep your exercising session quite short. It is very easy to pull a muscle when you should be toning it. Some exercises can be done without assistance—such as head and arm circling—but if you are planning to try out "Around the World" you must have someone with you to hold the horse. And, of course, always keep your hat on.

❶ Take your feet out of your stirrups and drop the reins. Swing one leg over the horse's neck so that you are sitting sideways.

❷ Now swing the other leg over the horse's rump so that you are facing backward. Be careful not to kick the horse with your heel.

❸ Continue "Around the World" until you end up in your original position. With practice, you will be able to carry out the whole exercise very quickly.

I was busy touching my toes this morning when Oscar put his head down—I fell off! That makes twice in one week!

The aids

A rider communicates with her horse using natural and sometimes artificial aids. The natural aids are the voice, body, legs, and hands. The artificial ones are the whip, spurs, and martingale. Stick to the natural aids to begin with and introduce the artificial ones as you become more experienced.

BODY, LEGS, AND HANDS

The body really means your body weight. It is an effective aid when used properly. Novice riders should not try to use their body weight as a signal until they can keep perfectly still in the saddle. Legs and hands are also extremely important. Your hands communicate directly with the horse's mouth, and your legs tell your horse whether you want it to turn right or left, go faster, slow down, or stop.

Outside leg
When moving in a straight line, your legs should be at the horse's sides with a gentle but even contact. When turning a corner, your outside leg should apply pressure behind the girth.

girth

Inside leg
The main function of your inside leg is to apply pressure to make your horse move forward. Apply extra pressure when you make a turn so that your horse bends his whole body.

Inside rein
Your hands keep contact with the horse's mouth at all times, and should follow the natural movement of the horse's head. Pressure on the inside rein shows the direction in which you want the horse to go. "Changing the rein" means changing direction.

There was an awful girl in my riding lesson today. She was just dragging poor Pedro around the ring. He was not happy!

14

VOICE CONTROLS

Always use your voice to give simple commands, whether you are riding or leading your horse. "Walk on" and "halt" are used everywhere, and your horse will quickly learn them.

SPURS

Spurs are used to reinforce the leg aids, but they should be used only by experienced riders. They should be blunt and made of metal.

Thursday
My Dad bought me a new whip. It is very sharp, with a silver-colored knob at the top. I was really pleased and gave him a big hug. I didn't tell him that actually I don't need a whip because Oscar always obeys my legs. At least, I think he is doing what he's told and not just following Annabel's pony.

Always Remember:

Carry your whip in your inside hand when riding around a school (arena). You should transfer it to your other hand when changing the rein (changing direction). It is the most important of the artificial aids and the one most usually used by a beginner. Its purpose is to reinforce the leg aids, and you should only use it when your horse doesn't respond to your leg.

running martingale

standing martingale

MARTINGALES

Both running and standing martingales are used to stop a horse carrying its head too high. They should be fitted so that they only have an effect when the horse raises its head to an angle at which you can't control it. Martingales must not be too short, as this can bruise the horse's mouth.

The gaits

Horses and ponies have four distinct gaits: walk, trot, canter, and gallop. At each gait, the rider's position is slightly different. Whatever your horse is doing and however fast it is traveling, you should keep your body relaxed and your joints supple. If you are stiff or tense, both you and your horse will feel uncomfortable.

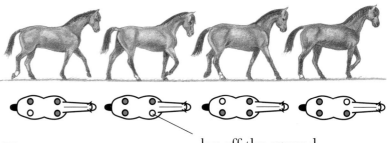

leg off the ground

THE WALK

The walk is a four-beat gait and the feet hit the ground in a regular order. You can count the footfalls—one-two-three-four. Your body should stay still except for a slight movement at your hip and waist. The horse nods its head in the walk, and your hands should "give" with the movement.

Always Remember:

Change the diagonal from time to time when you are doing the rising trot. This means staying in the saddle for one beat so that if you have been rising on the right diagonal you are now rising on the left. This can prevent your horse from becoming stiff on one side. In a ring, you usually change the diagonal when you change the rein. Changing the diagonal is just as important when hacking.

WALK TO TROT

Squeeze your inside leg on the girth, and your outside leg behind the girth. Sit well down in the saddle on your seat bones, and let your hands "give" to allow your horse to move into trot.

Q Do you have to go up and down when you trot?

A No, the sitting trot is often used to improve a rider's position in the saddle. It means exactly what it says—you do not try to rise to the trot at all. You should only do this for short periods.

THE TROT

The trot is a two-beat gait and the horse's feet come down in diagonal pairs. If the trot is energetic, there is a moment when all four feet are off the ground together. Once you learn to rise in the stirrups and sit back in the saddle in rhythm with the horse's movement, you will find it much more comfortable.

There's a new horse in the yard. Its owner does a lot of dressage, and some people think they are good enough for the national team. I watched them schooling this morning and was very impressed. I never realized there were so many different types of trot—working (which I suppose is what Oscar and I do all the time), collected, medium, and extended. Perhaps Oscar and I should be a bit more ambitious!

Down
The rider sits down in the saddle as the horse is on the left diagonal —the near fore-leg and the off hindleg are on the ground at the same time.

Up
The rider comes out of the saddle as the horse's off foreleg and near hindleg touch the ground—the right diagonal.

❶

❷

THE CANTER

The canter is a three-beat gait. To keep a proper balance and rhythm when cantering in a circle, your horse should always lead with the inside leg. This pony is leading with its off-foreleg on the right rein.

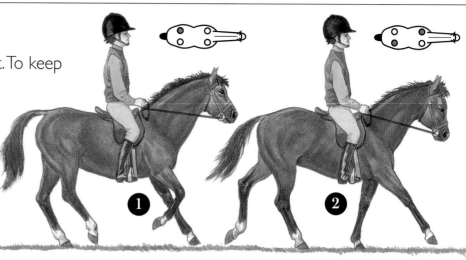

1   **2**

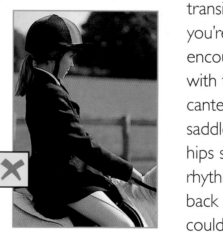

6 pm
We went out on my favorite ride today. It goes up a hill that we all call the Galloping Slope. It's a long grassy track that's flat to start with and then gets steeper. All the ponies know it and as soon as we get to the start, they're off!

TROT TO CANTER

To urge your horse into a canter, stop rising at the trot, sit down, and give the correct aids—inside leg pressure on the girth and outside leg pressure behind the girth.

You will find it easier to make the transition from trot to canter when you're on a bend. This also encourages the horse to strike off with the correct leading leg. At the canter, you should sit well down in the saddle for all three beats. Keep your hips supple and let your body move in rhythm with your horse. Don't lean back as you go into the canter or you could fall off.

1   **2**

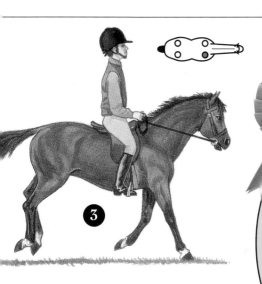

3

CANTER TO GALLOP

Gallop is a four-beat gait. To make it easier and less tiring for your horse, you should move your weight forward. Shift your weight on your knees and stirrups, and shorten your reins slightly to keep contact with your horse's mouth. Try to keep a straight line from your elbow, through your hand to the bit. Horses can get quite excited when they gallop, so you must be careful not to let the pace get out of hand.

Always Remember:
Check that your horse is cantering with the correct leg leading. To begin with, you may have to check by looking down, but as you get more experienced, you will be able to tell by the balance and rhythm of your horse. If you're on the wrong lead, go back to a trot, wait for the next bend, and ask again. Try to concentrate on giving the right aids.

I think I can finally tell which lead Oscar is cantering on without looking. Annabel and I tested each other— we did quite well!

Q Help! How do I slow down?

A To make the transition from a fast pace to a slower one, sit down in the saddle, increase the pressure of your lower legs, and at the same time apply additional pressure on the reins. The rider in the photo (above) is trying to slow down incorrectly and is not using his aids properly. Your horse should stay balanced and the transition should be smooth. In an emergency, turn your horse in an ever-decreasing circle until it is forced to slow down.

Gallop
In a gallop (below left to right) the rider's weight moves forward and is no longer in the saddle. Shortening your stirrup leathers can help you to balance. Your hands should move farther up the horse's neck and "give" with your horse's movement.

3

4

Schooling

The most important part of riding is schooling, or flatwork. When you train your horse to be balanced, flexible, and obedient, all your riding activities will improve. Half an hour of schooling on a regular basis will do wonders for any horse.

Circles

Circles are a useful way of assessing the flexibility and balance of a horse. In a standard ring (131 feet by 66 feet), ride a circle using half the ring. Your horse's body should follow the curve of the circle.

FLATWORK

It is safest for both you and your horse if schooling is carried out in an indoor ring. The idea is to get your horse moving rhythmically and in balance. It should carry its head in a natural position, have its weight correctly distributed, be energetic, and give an overall impression of balance and relaxation.

Serpentine

Gradually introduce serpentine movements, which test and improve the suppleness of your horse. Always keep your inside leg on the girth and your outside leg behind the girth to keep up the tempo of the movements.

Other figures

Smaller figures, such as those shown above, require greater flexibility. Your hips should be parallel with the horse's hindquarters, and your shoulders with the horse's shoulders.

LONGE TRAINING

This has two purposes. One is to exercise your horse if, for any reason, it cannot be ridden. The other is as part of its training. Longeing must be carried out correctly and should not be attempted by an inexperienced person except under strict supervision. If you are longeing, you stand in the center of a circle while the horse moves around you. You control your horse with your voice, a long longe line, which is attached to a longeing noseband on the horse's head, and a long longeing whip.

Sunday evening
We had a really tough schooling session today. I know it will make Oscar a better ride and me, I hope, a better rider, but I do find schooling sessions very tiring. Luckily it was Marty who was teaching—she's a really good teacher!

TROTTING POLES

These are useful when introducing your horse to jumping. They help to develop balance and rhythm, obedience, concentration, and coordination. Jumping poles make good trotting poles, because they are heavy enough not to roll if your horse touches them. The poles should be placed about 4 ^{1}/2 feet (135 cm) apart, or 3 ft 3 in (100 cm) if your pony is very small.

Always Remember:

Use all the aids when schooling. Many inexperienced riders forget that the voice is an important tool in training a horse. The only time that you are not allowed to use your voice is when you are doing a dressage test. Otherwise, the voice is excellent for calming an excited or nervous horse, and for giving orders.

Walking over poles
Start by showing your horse the poles to reassure it that they are nothing to be afraid of. After a while, it will walk quite happily beside you over the poles.

Riding over poles
Try to be relaxed when riding over trotting poles. Sit straight in the saddle and don't look down or hurry.

Jumping

All horses can jump, but not all of them want to. Some horses rely on their riders to tell them when to take off, others prefer to figure it out for themselves. Luckily, not many horses jump over their fences, even though they successfully clear greater heights out hunting or in the show ring.

When you first learn to jump you may find it easier to use a neck strap to hold onto. You can hold this through all five phases of the jump—approach, take-off, moment of suspension, landing, and the getaway.

Approach

1

Takeoff

2

Moment of suspension

3

1 Start by walking over two poles placed on the ground.

BUILDING UP

Once your horse will trot over poles on the ground, introduce some wings at each end of both poles. Then turn them into jumps, first by raising the second pole and then by raising both. Always approach jumps calmly and at an even gait. Do not introduce the second jump until your horse is moving smoothly and happily over the first.

2 Raise the second pole, leaving the first on the ground.

3 Raise both poles to form a combination fence.

I love jumping, even though I haven't done much of it yet —I think I will try out for the Olympics when I'm older!

22

1 Your position should be balanced, with your legs resting against the horse's sides and your hands in contact with the horse's mouth.

2 At takeoff, fold your body forward so that you take your weight off the horse's loins and are less likely to get "left behind."

POOR SEAT

Try not to stand up in the stirrups or to lean too far back. Concentrate on sitting centrally in the saddle, and use the neck strap to hold onto if you feel unsafe. It won't be long before your movements will automatically follow the horse's.

3 As the horse rounds its back, you should flatten yours, still leaning forward and still with your legs resting against the horse's sides. Keep looking in the direction you are going.

Landing

Getaway, or recovery

4 As the horse lands, allow it as much rein as it needs. Your body should become more upright. Once it has landed, take up the rein.

5 Remember—don't catch your horse in the mouth and don't land back in the saddle with a thump as you ride your horse forward.

Q Why does my horse sometimes stop or run around the jump?

A There are many reasons why horses fail to jump, but most of them are the fault of the rider. Don't jump the same jump over and over again as this will make your horse fed up. The only way it can tell you it's had enough is to refuse. It could be that you are asking your horse to jump something that is too big for it. You may have accidentally hurt your horse's mouth or landed heavily in the saddle, and it doesn't want it to happen again. Or it may be that you need to be more firm with your aids on the approach to the jump.

Saturday evening
Our trotting poles were being moved too easily in our lesson today, but Marty had a good idea. She made little piles of earth and rested the ends of each pole on the mounds, pushing them down quite firmly. Even when Oscar kicked one of the poles, it didn't move!

Types of jump

Jumps come in all shapes and sizes and can be portable or fixed. Show jumps, which are always portable, are usually colorful and highly decorated. Cross-country fences are usually solid, and are always fixed.

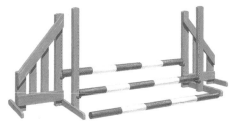

This is an ascending oxer, the easiest type of fence for your horse to jump.

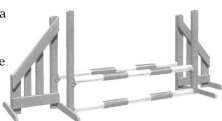

This is a pyramid fence, which, although wide at the base, is not difficult for your horse to jump.

2.30 pm—This morning we had a lesson in planning a show-jumping course. We learned that you should always place the first fence so that it is jumped toward the collecting ring, which is where the other horses would be at a show. Horses don't like jumping away from their friends!

This is a parallel jump. It must have a pole or filler under the front pole. This acts as a ground line to help your horse judge where to take off.

BASIC FENCES

There are four basic types of fence—upright, ascending oxer, pyramid, and parallel or square oxer. You can use them as single fences or combine them to form doubles or triples. Uprights include poles, gates, posts, and rails. Ascending oxers are triple bar fences or any twin-pole fence where the first bar is lower than the second. Pyramid fences are triangular in shape. Parallels have parallel poles with a plank or other pole underneath the front pole.

APPROACHING THE JUMP

You should approach whatever type of jump you are faced with at right angles, and head for the middle part. If you approach it from a sharp angle, your horse can not only run around the jump more easily, but may also find it harder to judge the takeoff.

SHOW JUMPING

At most shows, the jumping course features about eight or nine jumps in a figure-eight pattern. This includes one combination (two jumps usually set one stride apart), some spread jumps (ascending or square oxers), and some uprights.

CROSS-COUNTRY

Cross-country fences are solid and fixed and look more daunting than show jumps. However, most horses seem to enjoy jumping a cross-country course and jump obstacles that they would refuse or knock down in the show-jumping ring.
You won't be expected to jump into water until you are more experienced.

Q How do you keep score in show jumping?

A Penalties are given every time you make a mistake, and the winner is the rider who finishes the course with the lowest number of penalties.

Mistake	Penalties
• Knockdown of all or part of the fence	4
• 1st refusal or runout	3
• 2nd refusal or runout	6
• 3rd refusal or runout	Elimination
• 1st fall of horse or rider	8
• 2nd fall of horse or rider	Elimination
• Starting before the bell	Elimination
• Not going through the start gates	Elimination
• Leaving the arena	Elimination

Q How do you keep score in cross-country?

A Cross-country penalties are higher in value than show jumping penalties, but are not given as often.

Mistake	Penalties
• Starting before the signal to start	2
• 1st refusal or runout	20
• 2nd refusal or runout at the same jump	40
• 3rd refusal or runout at the same jump	Elimination
• Jumping a learner fence	15
• Fall of horse or rider	60
• 2nd fall of horse or rider	Elimination
• Going the wrong way around the course	Elimination
• Jumping a fence twice	Elimination
• Going on the wrong side of a boundary fence	Elimination
• Napping (misbehaving and not going in the direction you want) anywhere on the course	Elimination

Monday

Yesterday, Annabel and I went down a bridle path we'd never taken before. It led to a farmyard and as soon as we rode in, two dogs came out growling at us. We were so scared! Luckily the farmer came out and called them off. He wasn't very happy with us, though.

Hacking

One of the most enjoyable things about riding is going out for a hack. If you are lucky enough to live near countryside—open fields or forests—you probably have many rides to choose from. Hacking is also an excellent way of keeping your horse fit.

DIFFICULT GROUND

You should always carry a hoof pick in your pocket to remove stones and mud from your horse's hooves. Be careful on muddy ground as mud can be very deep and your horse's shoes may be sucked off. Also, beware of overhanging trees.

Q When hacking I've been told to follow the country code. What is the country code?

A The country code is the way that everyone using the countryside should try and behave.
You can't go wrong if you follow these simple guidelines:

- Always leave gates as you find them.
- Stick to bridle paths if you can.
- Do not ride across growing crops.
- Do not enter a field unless you know it is all right to do so.
- Avoid using very muddy tracks in wet weather.
- Be courteous to others at all times.
- Always slow down when meeting other riders or other users of the countryside.

MEETING PEDESTRIANS

You are likely to meet other people enjoying the countryside when hacking. Make sure you don't gallop past them as you could splash them with mud and frighten them. Always pass people at a walk, and treat them with the same respect that you would want them to show you.

 **①**

 **②**

 **③**

OPENING AND CLOSING A GATE

At some stage on your ride, you will probably have to pass through a gate. It saves time and trouble if you can train your horse to stand still while you unfasten the gate, back away while you open it, and go through quickly before the gate swings back. Make sure you close it properly behind you.

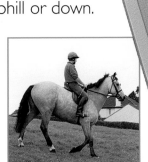

This shows the line you should take after going through a gate, so you can check that it is shut correctly.

UP AND DOWN HILLS

Riding up and down hills is ideal for getting your horse fit. Your position in the saddle is the same whether you are going uphill or down.

Your shoulders should always be in front of your hips. Do not lean back in the saddle when going downhill as this puts unnecessary strain on your horse's hindquarters.

Always Remember:

Walk for the last 10-15 minutes of any ride (about half a mile). This is particularly important if the ride has been a fast one and your horse is hot and sweaty. Horses need time to cool off gradually. Unless your pony is really tired, there is no need to get off and lead it, but if you do get off, you should run up the stirrups and loosen the girth.

Thursday
Oscar got a stone in his foot out riding today. I'd forgotten to bring a hoof pick with me and I couldn't get the stone out. It made him quite lame, so we were really late back. I got into real trouble, not because Oscar was lame, but because I had gone for a ride on my own without telling anyone where I was going.
Oops!

Riding on the road

From time to time, most riders have to take their horse or pony on the road. This can be very dangerous. Some motorists don't know how to deal with riders on the road, so all you can do is follow a few simple rules. Make sure you are doing everything you can to keep yourself and your horse safe.

TURNING

Turning right is the easiest maneuver you will have to make when riding on the road. You must follow normal traffic rules and ride on the right. To signal that you are going to make a right turn, simply put both reins in your left hand and extend your right arm outward. Always put your hand back on the rein before making the turn. Whenever you are on the road, you should obey traffic signals and road signs.

Q What else should I remember when I'm out on the road?

A • Ride single file on busy roads.
• On roads that are wide, straight, and quiet, you may ride two abreast.
• It is usually safest to stick to a walk on busy roads, but if you do have to trot, do not go faster than a working trot, and only do so in short bursts.
• Beware of slippery road surfaces.
• Keep to the right-hand side, even when you want to turn left. You can give a left-hand signal while riding on the right. Wait until you are level with the right-hand side of the crossroad before crossing the road. NEVER move into the middle of the road when waiting to turn.

COURTESY ON THE ROAD

As a rider, you should keep to the right side of the road, move in single file along busy roads and give clear signals at all times. Remember to thank other road users for their consideration.
You must not ride on footpaths, sidewalks, or trimmed grass shoulders. You can ride on rough shoulders, but be careful of hidden ditches or drains.

Tuesday
Oscar is so good on the roads and doesn't mind even the largest and noisiest truck. So I was really surprised this morning when he suddenly jumped at something in the hedge and leapt into the road. Luckily, nothing was coming!

HAND SIGNALS

All hand signals should be clear and held long enough to be seen and understood. Use the left and right arms to show in which direction you will be turning.

To slow traffic down, extend your arm and keep it rigid from shoulder to finger tips. Move your arm up and down several times.

To stop traffic, bend your arm and hold the palm of your hand toward the traffic. To stop traffic behind you, turn around in the saddle and use the same signal.

LEADING ON THE ROAD

If you have to lead your horse on the road, always place yourself between it and the traffic. You must still be on the right-hand side of the road, so you are leading your horse from the near, or left-hand, side. Make sure you can both be seen by wearing light-colored or fluorescent clothing.

Sunday
Annabel and I are taking a riding and road safety test. The instructor uses white tape to lay out an imaginary road and asks her friends to pretend to be hazards. It was interesting to see how the ponies reacted. Oscar was terrific as usual.

Always Remember:

Put a young, nervous, or inexperienced horse or rider in the middle of a group of riders when riding along a road. Having an experienced rider at the front keeps the pace steady. The rider at the back ensures that no one gets left behind. Stay in single file and do not crowd one another.

Quiz time

It's surprising how much you learn when you are doing things every day. Try the Quiz—and get your friends to try, too—and see what you can remember.

1 What are the natural aids?

2 What are the artificial aids?

3 What is the front part of the standing martingale fixed to?

4 Should your outside leg be on the girth or behind it?

5 Which hand carries the whip?

6 Is the walk a two-, three-, or four-beat gait?

7 Is the trot a two-, three-, or four-beat gait?

8 Is the canter a two-, three-, or four-beat gait?

9 When cantering in a circle, which leg should a horse always lead with?

10 Name the five phases of the jump.

11 Name four different types of jump.

Useful addresses

USA Pony Clubs
4041 Iron Works
   Parkway
Lexington, KY 40511-8462
www.ponyclub.org
Tel: (859) 254-7669

USA Equestrian, Inc.
4047 Iron Works
   Parkway
Lexington, KY 40511-8463
www.equestrian.org
Tel: (859) 254-2476

Evening
Mom has hinted that she might buy me a horse!! I'd miss Oscar loads but I'd still see him at the stables. I could enter so many shows on my own horse!

Answers
1 Legs, hands, body, voice. 2 Whip, martingale, spurs. 3 The noseband. 4 It should be behind it. 5 The inside hand if you're moving in a circle; whichever hand is most comfortable if you are moving in a straight line. 6 Four-beat. 7 Two-beat. 8 Three-beat 9 The inside leg. 10 Approach, take off, moment of suspension, landing, get-away or recovery. 11 Ascending oxer, pyramid, upright, parallel.

Glossary

aids
The means by which a rider communicates with a horse. These can be natural or artificial.

bit
A piece of tack attached to the reins that fits in the horse's mouth.

cantle
The highest part of the saddle at the back.

changing the rein
Changing the direction in which you ride around the ring (arena).

contact
The link, through the reins, between a horse's mouth and a rider's hands.

dock
The area under a horse's tail.

dressage
Exercises performed on flat ground to show the obedience, agility and suppleness of a horse.

fetlock joints
The joint that sticks out just above the hoof.

foal
A newborn horse or pony (up to 12 months).

gaits
The movements made naturally by a horse—the walk, trot, canter, and gallop.

girth
The wide strap that holds the saddle on.

hack
A ride out on a horse or pony.

laminitis
Sore feet, usually caused by overeating.

martingale
The straps that stop a horse from putting its head too high in the air for the rider to be able to have any control.

napping
Describes a horse being stubborn and refusing to go in the right direction.

pommel
The front, raised part of the saddle.

refusal
When a pony stops in front of a jump instead of jumping over it.

seat
The position in which you sit in the saddle. You should be able to draw a vertical line through your ear, shoulder, hip, and heel when your position is correct.

stirrup leathers
The straps that hold the stirrup irons onto the saddle.

stirrup irons
The two metal loops attached to the stirrup leathers that a rider's feet go in.

suspension (moment of)
When all four of the horse's feet are off the ground.

transition
The change from one gait to another.

Index

Photo credits
Abbreviations: l-left, r-right, b-bottom, t-top, c-center, m-middle
Front & back cover, 5tl, 6bl, 7tm, 8bl, 9bl, 9mr, 11tl, 12tr, 12bl, 12bm, 13 all, 15ml, 20tr, 22m all, 23m both, 23bm, 30ml, 31c, 32c— Select Pictures. 3b, 25 both—Corel. 4-5, 5br, 6br all, 9c, 10 all, 11c, 11mr, 11ml, 11bm, 11br, 12rb, 17ml, 18c, 21br all, 22bl all, 31bl, 32br—Aubrey Wade. 1, 4 both, 7lt, 8c, 14bl, 15tl, 15c, 15bl, 18mr, 19mr, 20br, 21t, 23bl, 24c, 26-27 all, 28-29 all—Kit Houghton Photography.
With many thanks to the Pony Club and the children at South Brockwells Farm, Sussex, England.